£3.49 0
428.6
KEt
(D22)

First I win a contest that
makes me a TV star.
Then I get to do some of
the most awesome extreme
sports in the world. And my
two best friends get
to come along for the ride.
How lucky am I?

First published in Great Britain in 2005 by
RISING STARS UK LTD.
76 Farnaby Road, Bromley, BR1 4BH

First published in Australia by Scholastic Australia in 2004.
Text copyright © Philip Kettle, 2004.

A Black Hills book, produced by black dog books

Designed by Blue Boat Design
Cover photo: Blue Boat Design

For more information visit our website at:
www.risingstars-uk.com

British Library Cataloguing in Publication Data

A CIP record for this book is available from the British Library

ISBN 1 905056 43 5

Printed by Bookmarque Ltd, Croydon, Surrey

THE XTREME WORLD OF BILLY KOOL

by Phil Kettle

book:04
snowboarding

RISING STARS

CONTENTS

SNOWBOARDING EQUIPMENT

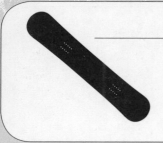

Snowboard

Snowboards are made from a polyethylene called P-Tex. It is very durable and flexible.

Bindings

Bindings attach your snowboarding boots tightly to the board so you can control how it moves.

Boots

Snowboarding boots are locked into place by the bindings. They are waterproof and very sturdy.

Goggles

Goggles protect your eyes from the sun, which reflects off the snow. They also keep snow out of your face.

Gloves

Thermal gloves will keep your hands from getting too cold.

Trousers

Snowboarding trousers are waterproof. They will keep you warm and protect you if you fall.

Jacket

Waterproof thermal jackets keep you warm and also allow your skin to breathe.

NATHAN

I could tell there was something wrong with Nathan. He's my best friend. And the thing about best friends is that you always know when they're acting weird. He didn't seem to be sick or anything like that. It was more like something was bugging him.

Sally, Nathan and I were the envy of every kid at school. We should have been on a high. We'd gone bungy jumping a few weeks ago,

and whitewater rafting a couple
of weeks before that, and this
coming weekend we were going
snowboarding.

The TV ratings for *The Xtreme
World of Billy Kool* were excellent. We
were getting lots of fan mail that we
tried to answer every week. There
were hundreds of letters. Some
of them were sprayed with really
smelly perfume. Lots of people
asked how they could come on the
show. Sally's mum and my dad
helped us keep track of the mail.

Nathan's sister Crystal had said
hello to me twice this week and
she'd even called me by my name.
I had a French test and passed it.

My French teacher, Mrs Crabtree, had even written in bright red pen, 'a much improved result—well done'. Hopefully that meant my parents would stop hassling me so much about my homework.

So my life was awesome, and Nathan's should have been too. But there was something wrong with him and I didn't know what it was.

I decided the best way to find out was to ask. If your best mate couldn't ask what was wrong, then who could?

Sally, Nathan and I walked home from school. We ran past the fence where the monster lived, just like we do every afternoon after school.

As usual he roared and we ran away laughing. But today Nathan didn't laugh and he didn't run either.

I decided that when I got home I'd have something to eat, then I'd go to Nathan's house and try to find out what was up.

WHAT'S THE PROBLEM!

I pressed the doorbell. Nathan's mum answered. I asked her if I could see Nathan.

'He's in his bedroom,' Nathan's mum said. I'd been hoping that Crystal would answer the door, but she was nowhere to be seen.

Nathan was lying on his bed when I went into his room.

'So, Nathan, what's happening?'

'Nothing,' he said.

'If there's nothing going on, why are you in such a bad mood?'

'Who said that I'm in a bad mood?'

'You've been acting like you're in a bad mood.'

Nathan looked up, picked up his miniature basketball and threw it at the basketball ring above his bedroom door. 'Three points.'

Then he just stared at the wall. 'My dad is coming to see me on Sunday,' he said.

Nathan's father hadn't lived in the same house as Nathan for a long time. I thought that Nathan would have been pleased to see him.

I never really thought about what it would be like not having my dad around. It was just something that I never had to consider. But there

were a lot of kids at school whose
mums or dads didn't live with them.

I didn't know what to say to
Nathan, so I changed the subject.
'Have you read the running sheet for
snowboarding on Saturday? We've
got half a day to practise boarding
and jumps before we start shooting.'

Nathan looked at me for moment,
then spoke. 'I haven't spoken to my
dad for a year and I haven't seen
him for two years. The last time I
spoke to him, I asked if I could see
him, and he told me he was really
busy and maybe I could come and
visit him some other time.'

I didn't say anything. I thought it
was better to let him talk.

'He left us and moved to another town. He's got another family now. He probably only wants to see me now because I'm on TV!'

Nathan took a deep breath, picked up the basketball from the floor, ran toward the door and slam-dunked the ball straight through the hoop. 'If he thinks I'm going to be nice to him, he can think again.'

I left Nathan's place without saying
anything about his dad. I really
didn't know what to say.

I dropped into Sally's house on
my way home. She always seems to
know what to do and what to say.
Or at least, she thinks she does!

Sally reckoned all kids think their
parents are okay and all parents
think their kids are okay. Parents
might not like what we do sometimes
and we might not like what they

do, but that doesn't stop them from liking us or us liking them.

I sometimes think my parents don't like me very much—especially when they make me do something that I don't want to do…like eat brussel sprouts!

When I told Sally that, she frowned and said that wasn't exactly what she meant. I knew that too, but I couldn't think of another example.

I reckon that Nathan's dad thinks that Nathan is cool, but how would Nathan know that if he never saw his dad?

Sally said she would ring Shey that night. Shey had told us that if we ever had a problem we should ring her. I didn't know how Shey could help, but I didn't have any better ideas.

CAST AND CREW MEETING

Nathan's mood had improved a bit by the time we were in the limo being taken to the cast and crew meeting. Nathan said his dad had taken him out for dinner. Even though he was still kind of mad, I knew straight away that whatever they had to eat, it mustn't have been brussel sprouts.

Nathan said that he and his dad had a really big fight at the restaurant and some of the other people in the restaurant had stared at them. Nathan said that after the fight they had both calmed down a bit. He'd told his dad exactly what he thought about everything, and that taking him out for dinner didn't count for anything. His dad said that he understood what Nathan was saying and that he was going to try and spend more time with him.

I was thinking that I was really glad my dad lived with me. Nathan said that he really wanted to believe his dad but he would just have to wait and see. Sally had a funny look on her face, but I couldn't ask her what was going on because she was already getting out of the limo.

'Hi, guys,' the director said when we walked into the meeting room.

We said hello to him and all the crew. It felt like we were really getting to know them. They were starting to feel like family now, but the best thing about them was that they didn't make you eat brussel sprouts or come into your room without knocking first.

'Alright, people,' the director said. 'Here's the plan of action. Tomorrow morning at 7 a.m. the limo will pick up Billy, Sally and Nathan and take them to the helipad. We'll all meet there, then we're flying by helicopter to the snow. We'll do some practice runs in the morning, then we'll shoot after lunch. The camera crew will stay up for a few more days to get some location shots. Has everyone got that?'

We all nodded.

'We'll get you kitted out in snow gear when we get there, but dress warm anyway. The snow's looking good. It looks like some more will fall tonight. Okay, last but not least, your show got more fan mail this week than any other show.' The director emptied a sack of letters onto the table. Letters poured out.

'You're kidding,' Nathan said.

'No. You're famous,' the director said. 'You'd better get used to it.

Here's one for you, Nathan. It's from a girl.'

The director read it out.

To Nathan

I think that your show is really cool. I really love extreme sports - I go rock climbing every weekend. After school I climb on the bluestone wall near my house. You have to get across it without falling off. If you ever need someone to come on your show, I could come.

Thanks from one of your fans,

Eloise

PS I think that you are cute.

All the crew started cheering and teasing Nathan. Nathan looked happier than he had all week.

When we got to the helipad,
Nathan's dad was waiting with Shey.
'Surprise!' they both said.

'I was talking to your dad on
the phone the other night and he
told me he used to be a bit of a
snowboarder,' Shey said. 'I invited
him along to give you lessons.'

Nathan and his dad sat next to
each other on the helicopter. I was
trying to listen in, but it was too
hard to hear them over the noise

of the helicopter and Sally kept elbowing me. Riding in a helicopter is a bit scary to start with, but once you get used to it, it's like going on a ride at a theme park. We were flying over roads and mountains. Sally elbowed me again and pointed. We were nearly there. I've never seen so much white altogether at the same time. It would be really bad if you wore white clothes—nobody would see you.

Nathan was looking pretty pleased when we got to the snowfields.

They gave us really cool clothes to put on—base layers and mid layers and waterproof snowboard trousers and jackets, goggles and boots and gloves. I couldn't wait to see how good we looked on TV. I wondered if Crystal liked snowboarders.

Nathan's dad had his own snowboarding gear. Shey told us that he had won a lot of snowboarding events and was a really good snowboarder.

'I haven't snowboarded for years,' Nathan's dad said.

'It'll come back quickly,' Shey said.

Soon we were out on the snow. Nathan's dad showed us heaps of moves. If it wasn't for him, there's no way we would have been good enough to snowboard for the show.

'If you're half as good as your dad, you'll be really good,' Sally said.

'I hope it runs in the family,' Nathan said.

For four hours we cratered into snowbanks, punched the snow, flailed and bailed—these are all really cool words for landing face first into the snow. It's lucky snowboarders have got so many words to describe stacking, because we were doing heaps of it!

We were just getting the hang of it when shooting was due to start. All the camera crew were wearing heaps of clothes. At least we got to snowboard to keep warm. All they were doing was shooting footage of us. It was freezing up there.

Location Map

(6)

(headphones icon)

Our Equipment

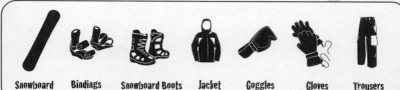

| Snowboard | Bindings | Snowboard Boots | Jacket | Goggles | Gloves | Trousers |

1. Helicopter drop off point on mountain peak

2. Steep descent down mountain

3. Snow mound jump for big air

4. Bumps in the snow known as moguls

5. Hand rail for rail slide stunts

6. Sound crew based for monitoring

LIGHTS, CAMERA, ACTION

BILLY
Good afternoon and welcome to *The Xtreme World of Billy Kool*. My name is Billy Kool. I'm the host of this awesome show. Today we are standing on top of a snow-covered slope, about to go snowboarding. With me are my co-hosts, Sally and Nathan.

SALLY
Snowboarding is one of the best extreme sports!

NATHAN
Yep, we're going to have heaps of fun today. We've been trying moves all morning. I reckon I could beat you any day.

SALLY
Yeah, right. Whatever!

BILLY
Well, I think I'll be
better than both of you.
But while we're arguing
about that, we have with
us, as usual, Shey. Shey
is an expert in extreme
sports and is going to
give us a few tips about
snowboarding.

SHEY
Good afternoon, Billy,
Sally and Nathan. As you
can see we are dressed in
the right clothes. That's
really important because
it's so cold up here.

SALLY
The boys look like they're

about to walk on the moon. We're wearing three layers—a base layer next to our skin, a mid-layer and an outer layer of trousers and a jacket. The outer layer is made out of waterproof fabric that also breathes, so we don't get too hot.

NATHAN
We're warm-that's really important when you're in the snow. We're going to put on gloves, goggles and a helmet. We're also going to wear wrist guards because so many snowboarders hurt their wrists by putting out their hands when they're trying to stop.

SHEY
Today we are going to go down a 35° slope and do some tricks on the way to the bottom.

NATHAN
I'm going to be really good at this.

SALLY
The moves that you pull when you're snowboarding are a cross between skateboarding and surfing.

BILLY
I'm really good at surfing and skating.

SHEY
Then it's time for everyone watching to see how good you really are.

SALLY
But before we start we
have to strap our feet
into the snowboards.

NATHAN
Now that we've done that,
we just need to pull our
goggles down over our eyes
and we're ready to go.

BILLY
We've decided that Nathan
is going to go first.

NATHAN
Who decided?

BILLY
I did!

NATHAN
How come I have to
go first?

BILLY
Because you said you were going to be the best. And I thought that I might be able to learn from you.

NATHAN
Yeah, right!

SALLY
Well, hurry up or all our viewers will go to sleep.

The cameras shoot the steepness of the slope.

SHEY
The slope is covered in powder snow. That's snow that has just fallen and is really soft and light.

NATHAN
That's good. If you crash it won't hurt as much!

SALLY
So are you ready to go?

NATHAN, BILLY, SALLY and SHEY are wired for sound. They are able to talk to each other as they go down the slope.

BILLY
We're watching Nathan as he pushes off. He's had a good start.

SALLY
I wonder how far he'll go before he falls.

NATHAN
I've got loads of speed. This is crazy.

BILLY
Well, it's time that you

showed us some tricks. We want to see if you can get air.

NATHAN
I'm headed for a mound in the snow. I'll do a jump.

Nathan hits the mound and launches himself into the air. He looks really good and gets loads of air. But then it starts to go horribly wrong.

SALLY
Oh-oh.

NATHAN
Aaaaaaaahhhhhhh! I'm going to crash.

Nathan lands in the snow and is buried up to his shoulders.

SALLY
Are you alright?

NATHAN
Well, I think I am. But I
won't know for sure until
I get all this snow off
my face. I really punched
the snow!

BILLY
More like the snow punched
you. That was the best
fall I've ever seen.

*Nathan stands up and wipes
the snow from his face.*

NATHAN
I feel fine. At least the
snow was soft to land in.
But snow doesn't taste
that good and it really
is cold.

SHEY
Now that we know Nathan is okay, it's time that Billy and Sally showed us how good they are. Are you ready?

SALLY
I'm ready. Billy, are you ready to go?

BILLY
I'm going to go so fast the snow will melt!

SALLY
Whatever.

Billy and Sally push off. They both seem to be doing really well.

BILLY
This is cool! Now I'm going to try a 360.

NATHAN
I hope you like the taste
of snow more than I do.

SALLY
I'm just going to keep
going as fast as I can.
I want to make it to the
bottom of the slope.

*Billy lifts into the air
and starts to turn the
board. Billy looks really
good in the air. But
like Nathan he loses his
balance and ends up face-
down in the snow.*

BILLY
I think I might have tried
to pull a move that only
a pro snowboarder could
do. Maybe I'm on my way to
becoming professional.

NATHAN
I hope a dog hasn't done
something on that snow you
just got a mouthful of.

BILLY
Same!

SALLY
Well, while both of you
crashed, I've made it
to the bottom of the run
and proved to everyone
watching that I am the
best snowboarder!

BILLY
I think that Nathan and I
were just a bit unlucky.

NATHAN
Yeah, but we were keen to
try and do some tricks.
You just went in a

straight line. That's not hard.

SALLY
Maybe, but I made it to the bottom!

SHEY
While Billy, Nathan and Sally are making their way back to the top of the slope, I am going to introduce you to one of the world's great snowboarders. It is my pleasure to introduce you to John 'Snowflake' Arnold.

SNOWFLAKE
Hi, Shey.

Billy, Nathan and Sally arrive back.

SNOWFLAKE
I watched you guys go down
the slope. With a lot of
practice you could all be
good snowboarders.

BILLY
I could be a champion.
What do you think?

SNOWFLAKE
Well, as I said, with a
lot of practice I think
you could have some
potential.

SALLY
How did you get your
nickname, Snowflake?

SNOWFLAKE
I got it because I float
through the air like a
snowflake.

NATHAN
What's the best thing
about being a champion
snowboarder?

SNOWFLAKE
Snowboarding is a huge
adrenaline rush. The
feeling of flying through
the air and inventing new
tricks is fantastic.

SALLY
Now that you have seen
Nathan and Billy, who are
not so great, we're going
to watch Snowflake and see
how a champion snowboards.

BILLY
While we're watching
Snowflake show us how
to snowboard, we'll say
goodbye. This has been

The Xtreme World of Billy Kool. I hope that you enjoyed today's show. Please tune in again next week for another exciting show. Until then, I'm Billy Kool and you're not.

DIRECTOR
Cut! That's a wrap. Great show, well done.

BILLY
Let's do another run.

SALLY
I bet I can beat you to the bottom. Are you coming, Nathan?

NATHAN
I'm going snowboarding with Dad. We're going to stay up here for the rest of the weekend.

NATHAN'S DAD walks up.

NATHAN'S DAD
Good show!

NATHAN
Yeah, except the bit where I crashed.

NATHAN'S DAD
Do you want to have another go at that jump?

NATHAN
I wouldn't mind. See you later, Billy and Sally.

BILLY AND SALLY
Bye!

THE WRAP UP

It's been a really big week.
Snowboarding is awesome. I had a
fantastic time in the snow. Snow is
really cold and wet. I wouldn't want
to live in the snow all the time, but
it's really good fun to visit.

Nathan's dad is really cool at
snowboarding! Nathan reckons
that his father is probably the best
snowboarder in the world.

Well, I reckon that one day I
might be the world's best. But at the

moment I would be pleased to be as good as Nathan's dad.

Nathan came over to my place when he got home from snowboarding. He had a really big smile on his face. He told me that his dad is going to spend more time with him. When they were snowboarding, Nathan's dad said that he was sorry that he hadn't been around much. He asked Nathan if he wanted to spend the next school holidays with him. They might go whitewater rafting together, or bungy jumping. His dad is really into the idea of trying more extreme sports.

Maybe if they go whitewater

rafting, Dad and I could go too.

I guess that Nathan felt hurt by his dad. But I'm sure that Nathan really loves his dad and now they are on the way to being best friends again.

Most of my homework is done. My mum told me that I have to clean my bedroom this week. I really hate cleaning my room. I never know where to find anything after I have cleaned up.

I am so lucky that I won the extreme sport contest. Extreme sports are really cool!

Dear Billy,

I think you, Nathan and Sally are awesome. I watch your show all the time. I did something really extreme last week – I broke both my legs skiing. All my friends think I'm really cool, just like you. And everyone has signed my cast. I can't wait for my legs to get better so I can go skiing again. You can come too if you want.

Jodie, your fan

Extreme Information

History

One of the first snowboards was made in 1929 by M. J. Burchett. It was made out of plywood and the snowboarder's feet were secured to the board with a piece of clothesline and horse's reins.

It wasn't until thirty years later, in the mid-1960s, that the next prototype was made by Sherman Poppen, an engineer in the United States. He made it as a present for his daughter. It was called a 'Snurfer', which reflects how much snowboarding resembles surfing (and skateboarding).

The Snurfer was made by binding two skis together and putting a rope at the nose, so the rider could hold the Snurfer and keep it more stable.

Dimitrije Milovich started making snowboards in 1969. He came up with the idea for his boards after sliding down some hills on a cafeteria tray in college.

Jake Burton invented the first bindings for snowboards.

As snowboarding became more popular in the 1970s and 1980s, new designs for snowboards and new materials were developed and soon snowboards were invented that were like the ones that are used today.

When snowboarding first started, skiers thought that it was silly. Snowboarders often weren't allowed to use ski-lifts with skiers or the ski trails. This meant that

snowboarding had to be done off-piste
(off the beaten track). Skiers thought that
snowboarding would never last, but it has
become more and more popular. Now it
is one of the most popular extreme sports.
It's predicted that more people will be
snowboarding than skiing in ten years.

Glossary

Airdog

A snowboarder who does a lot of aerial tricks and jumps.

Bail

A term used to describe crashing or falling.

Beat

A term that means something isn't good.

Bonk

To hit something, like the edge of a halfpipe, really hard.

Bust

To get huge air.

Chatter

When a snowboard shakes a lot on turns

or at high speed. Snowboarders try to stop their boards from 'chattering' so they have more control.

Crater

A crash or fall.

Cruiser run

Snowboarding down a smooth and relaxed run. Very little difficulty.

Goofy

Riding with the right foot in front.

Grommet

A young snowboarder who is really into snowboarding.

Jib

Riding on something other than snow, eg, trees, logs, stair rails.

Poser

A poser is someone who is pretending to

be better than they really are.

Punch

A way to describe a very bad crash.

Rolling down the windows

A term that describes what happens when
snowboarders lose their balance and
start to rotate their arms to try and stay
upright.

Sick

A term that means something is really
good.

Snake

Someone who cuts in front of you when
you are waiting for the ski-lift, or who
drops into the halfpipe in front of you.

Stoked

To be very excited.

Equipment

Snowboard

A snowboard is made up of different layers. The inner core is made from aluminium, wood or foam, which is strengthened with a fibreglass coating on either side. The logo or design on the top of the board is sealed with a transparent topcoat. The underneath of the board is covered with a clear polyethylene material called P-Tex. Snowboards are both durable and flexible. There are different sorts of boards: alpine, freestyle and freeride.

Alpine Snowboards

Alpine boards are also called race boards and carving boards. They are

good for speed and racing, and allow
snowboarders to make fast, sharp turns.

Freestyle Snowboards

Freestyle boards are built for performing
tricks: spins, air and riding backwards
(fakie). Snowboarders use freestyle
boards in the halfpipe. The boards are
easy to turn and very responsive.

Freeride Snowboards

Freeride boards are the most popular
snowboard. They can go anywhere and
can be used on any part of the mountain.
They are long enough to do neat turns
like an alpine board, and are flexible
enough to do tricks like a freestyle board.

Boots

Alpine boots are made out of hard plastic
with straps that can be done up. Soft

boots are used for freestyle or freeriding. They're made from rubber and leather.

Binding

Step-in binding is the latest development in binding technology. It allows snowboarders to lock into the binding just by stepping onto the board. To get out, there is a catch release. Alpine boards use a plate binding, made from metal. A front clip fastens the boot. Freestyle bindings hold soft boots in place with straps tightened by clips.

PHIL KETTLE

Phil Kettle lives in inner-city Melbourne, Australia. He has three children, Joel, Ryan and Shey. Originally from northern Victoria, Phil grew up on a vineyard. He played football and cricket and loved any sport where he could kick, hit or throw something.

These days, Phil likes to go to the Melbourne Cricket Ground on a winter afternoon and cheer on his favourite Australian Rules team, the Richmond Tigers. Phil hopes that one day he will be able to watch the Tigers win a grand final — 'Even if that means I have to live till I'm 100.'

THE Xtreme WORLD OF BILLY KOOL

by Phil Kettle

Billy Kool books are available
from most booksellers.
For mail order information
please call Rising Stars on
01933 443862 or visit
www.risingstars-uk.com